ZOOTOPIA
POLICE
FRIENDS OF THE MARKET
Z
ZOOTOPIA'S OLDEST FELLOWSHIP
LIFE ON THE WILD SIDE
the Dive Bar AND LOUNGE
VOLT VIPER
ALL DISTRICTS
THE TUBES
TRANSIT SYSTEM
The Shell HUT
GRAND ESTATE
PELTER MANOR
TUNDRATOWN
ZOOTOPIA
POLICE
ZOOTOPIA
POLICE
MMFE
BONUS PISCIS MORTUUS EST PISCIS

How many different words can you make using the letters in:

NEVER OUTFOXED

ANSWERS INCLUDE: DEVOUR, FORTUNE, FOUR, FRONT, OFTEN, REFUND, ROUND, TREND, TUXEDO, UNDER.

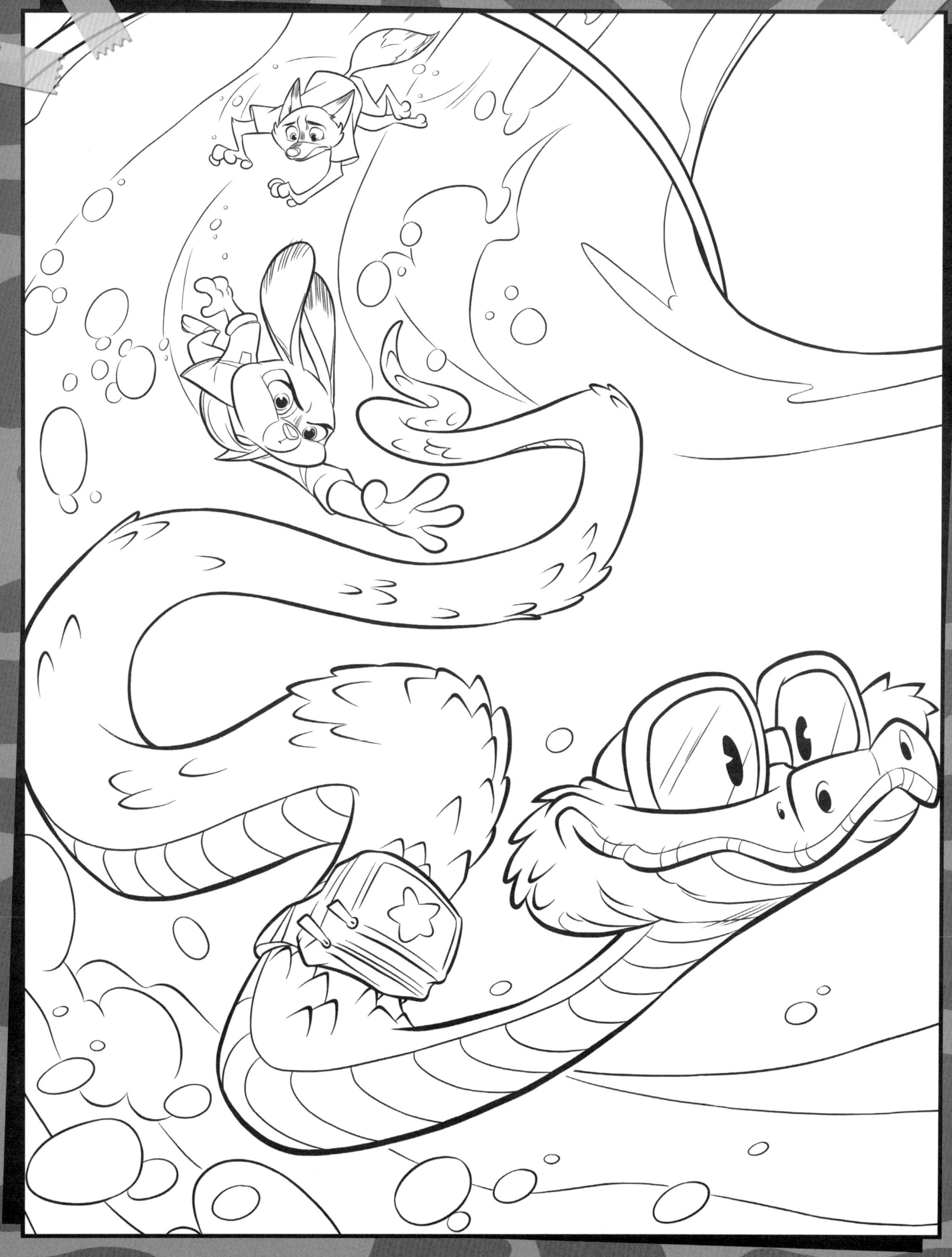

ANIMAL Alphabet

Mayor Winddancer wants to know how many animals you can name in a minute. Playing with a friend, take turns timing each other to see how many animals you can think of starting with different letters of the alphabet. The person who writes down the most animals wins. To get you started, there is an African squirrel called a Xerus!

A ____________________
B ____________________
C ____________________
D ____________________
E ____________________
F ____________________
G ____________________
H ____________________
I ____________________
J ____________________
K ____________________
L ____________________
M ____________________
N ____________________
O ____________________
P ____________________
Q ____________________
R ____________________
S ____________________
T ____________________
U ____________________
V ____________________
W ____________________
XERUS ________________
Y ____________________
Z ____________________

A ____________________
B ____________________
C ____________________
D ____________________
E ____________________
F ____________________
G ____________________
H ____________________
I ____________________
J ____________________
K ____________________
L ____________________
M ____________________
N ____________________
O ____________________
P ____________________
Q ____________________
R ____________________
S ____________________
T ____________________
U ____________________
V ____________________
W ____________________
XERUS ________________
Y ____________________
Z ____________________

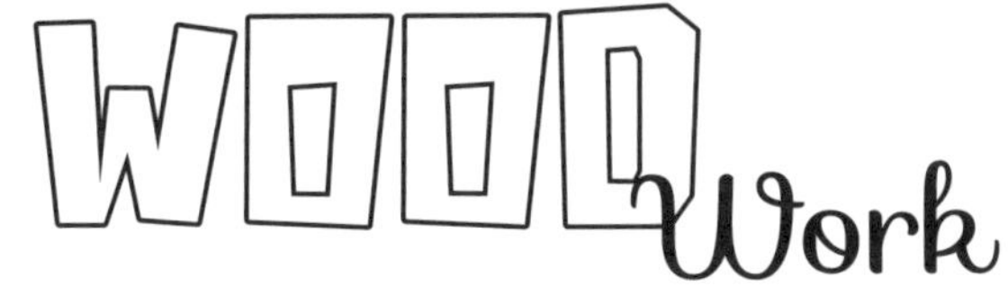

Work

Cross out the word WOOD every time you see it.
When you see a letter that is not part of the word,
write it in the spaces below to describe Nibbles Maplestick.

~~W O O D~~ G W O O D N W O O D A

W O O D W O O D W S W O O D

O W O O D M W O O D W O O D E

NIBBLES MAPLESTICK IS:

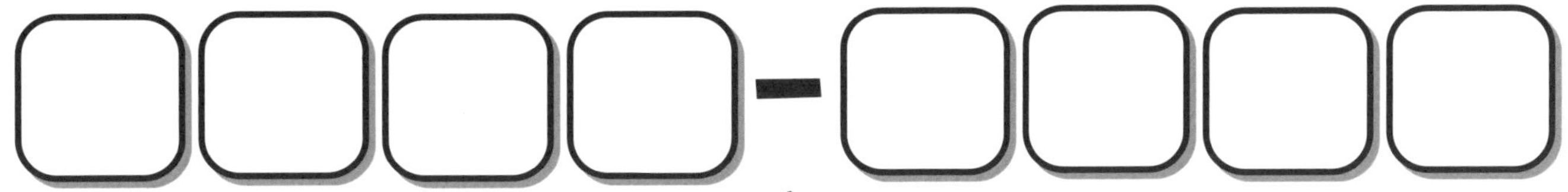

ANSWER: NIBBLES MAPLESTICK IS GNAW-SOME.

ANIMAL Artwork

There is a home for every type of animal in Zootopia. If you were an animal, what type do you think you'd be? Draw yourself as an animal below.

ONE IN A Gazellion

Gazelle has lots of imitators, but she's one of a kind.
Find the Gazelle that matches the bigger picture perfectly and circle it.

ANSWER: B IS THE MATCHING GAZELLE.

HIDDEN Letters

Nick and Judy look different. Are they hiding something? There are definitely some letters hiding in the image below. Find the ten hidden letters and rearrange them to figure out what the partners are up to.

THE HIDDEN LETTERS:

___ ___ ___ ___ ___ ___ ___ ___ ___ ___

NICK AND JUDY ARE:

___ ___ ___ ___ ___ ___ ___ ___ ___ ___

ANSWER: NICK AND JUDY ARE UNDERCOVER.

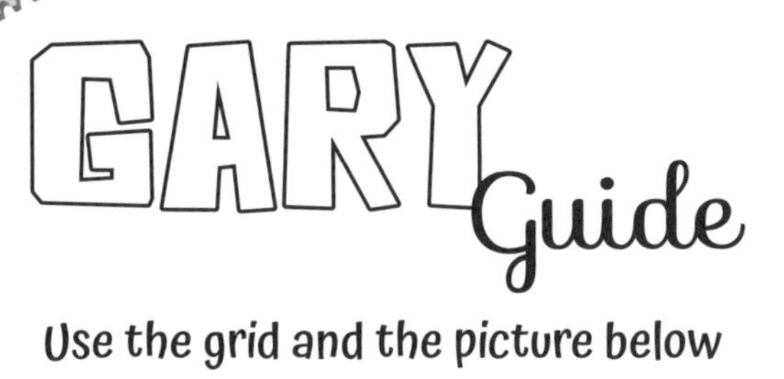

Use the grid and the picture below
to draw Gary De'Snake.

LYNX Links

Play with a friend, each using a different coloured pencil. Take turns drawing a line linking two dots together. You can only draw lines up and down, not diagonally. Try and link four dots together to make a box, then write your initial inside. After you've connected all the dots, count up your initials and whoever made the most boxes wins.

EXAMPLE

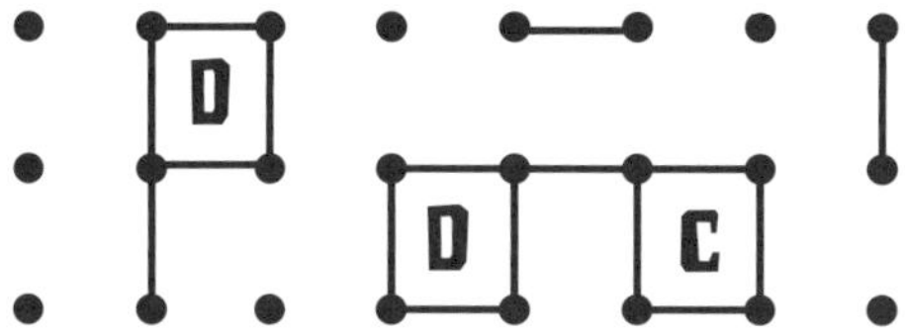

D D C

UNIFORM Inspections

Chief Bogo is doing a uniform inspection of the ZPD's Police Officers.
Help him by matching each detail to the character it belongs to and drawing a line between them.

ANSWER: 1—C; 2—B; 3—A; 4—D.

POLICE

MARSH Map

Nick and Judy are trying to get back to the entrance to the Marsh Market. Which paths gets them there stepping on the fewest walruses? Circle it below.

ANSWER: PATH C HAS THE FEWEST WALRUSES.

CODE Breaker

Use the ZPD code below to describe Judy.

C

I

O

S

H

M

P

T

JUDY IS:

ANSWER: JUDY IS HOP-TIMISTIC.

SNAKES and Ladders

Grab a friend, a die and cut out your player tokens. Start at 1, then role your die and move forwards that many spaces. If you land on a square that has Gary's mouth, follow it down the board. If you land on square at the base of a ladder, climb it up the board. The first player to reach square 25 wins!

PLAYER TOKENS

ASK AN ADULT FOR HELP!

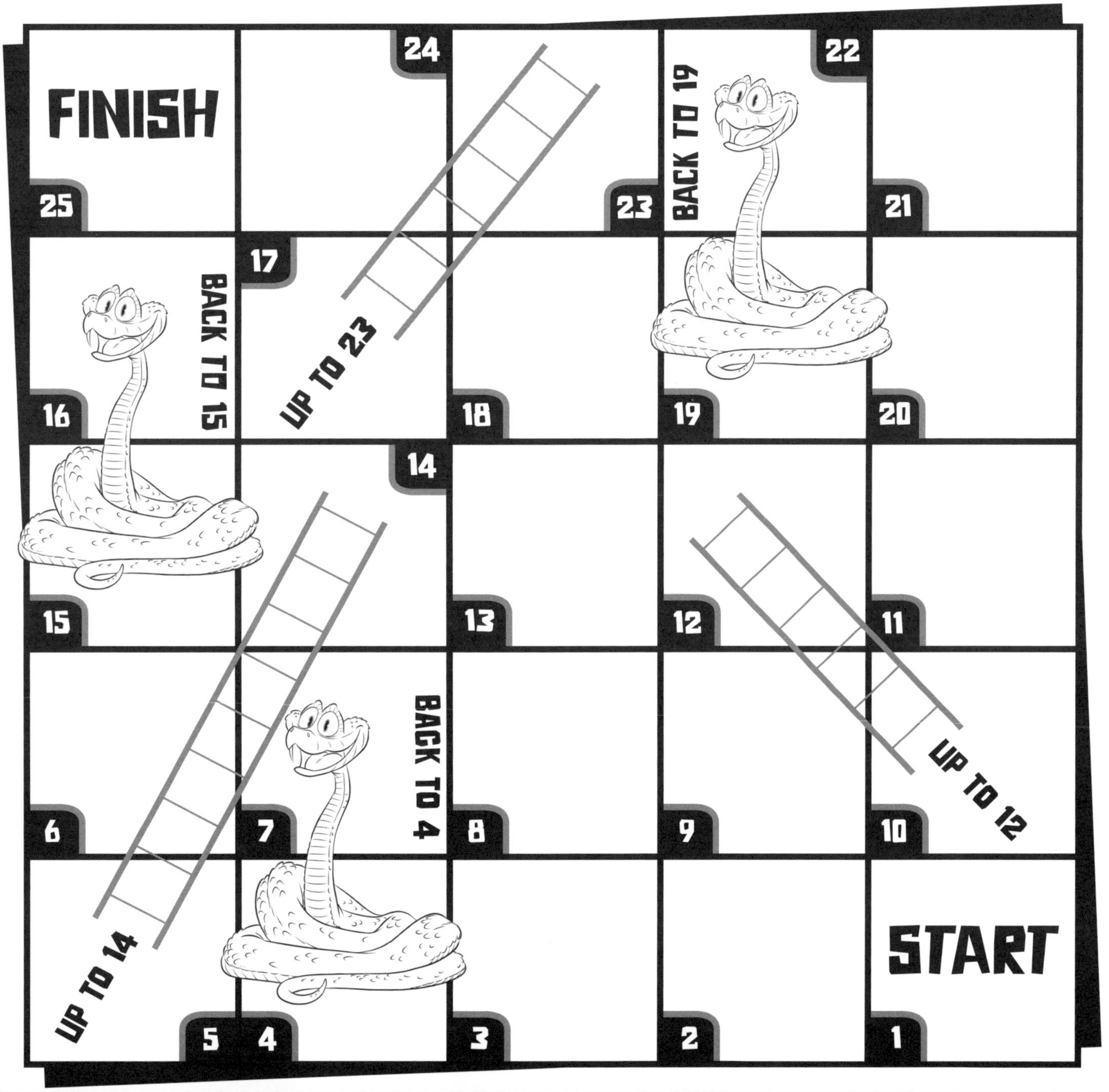

FINISH 25	24	23	22 BACK TO 19	21
16 BACK TO 15	17 UP TO 23	18	19	20
15	14	13	12	11
6	7 BACK TO 4	8	9	10 UP TO 12
5 UP TO 14	4	3	2	START 1